True Viticulture: Cultivatio
Grapevines"

Chapter 1: Introduction to Grapevine Cultivation

1.1 The History of Grape Cultivation

Welcome to the world of grapevines! I'm not just *a farmer, Sommelier, Gourmet, Grapevine Breeder*; I'm also deeply passionate about the art and science of grapevine cultivation. In this chapter, we embark on a journey through time to explore the fascinating history of grape cultivation.

From the ancient vineyards of Mesopotamia, where the first cultivated grapes were documented over 6,000 years ago, to the lush vineyards of modern-day Napa Valley, grape cultivation has a storied past. Grapes have been cherished for their culinary, medicinal, and, of course, winemaking qualities throughout history.

As we delve into this rich history, we'll discover how grape cultivation techniques have evolved, from the rudimentary methods of early civilizations to the sophisticated practices employed by today's viticulturists. Understanding this history not only connects us to our roots but also provides valuable insights into the enduring allure of grapevines.

1.2 Varieties of Grapevines

Now that we've stepped into the historical vineyards, let's turn our attention to the incredible diversity of grapevine varieties. As a grapevine enthusiast, I can attest to the sheer wonder of this diversity, which spans the globe and tantalizes the taste buds.

Grapes come in an astonishing array of colors, flavors, and characteristics. Whether you savor the bold richness of a Cabernet Sauvignon or the delicate aromatics of a Riesling, there's a grape variety to suit every palate and purpose.

As you journey through the pages of this chapter, you'll not only become acquainted with popular grape varieties but also gain insights into the uniqueness of each. From the classic Chardonnay to the lesser-known gems, these varieties are the building blocks of the viticultural world, each contributing its own charm to the vineyard tapestry.

1.3 Importance of Grapevine Cultivation

Grapevine cultivation isn't just about tending to vines; it's a cornerstone of agriculture and culture. Why, you ask? Well, let's uncork the bottle of knowledge and take a sip of understanding.

For starters, grapes are a high-value crop. The wine industry alone generates billions of dollars in revenue globally, supporting countless jobs, from grape growers and winemakers to hospitality and tourism. But it's not just about economics; grapes have a deeper significance.

Throughout history, grapes have been symbols of celebration, tradition, and community. The clinking of glasses during special occasions and the sharing of a bottle with friends and family are rituals that connect us to our roots and create lasting memories.

1.4 Climatic Considerations

Ah, the climate—a critical factor in the world of grapevine cultivation. From the sun-soaked slopes of California to the cooler terroirs of Burgundy, the climate plays a leading role in the life of a grapevine.

Grapes are discerning about where they grow. They thrive in specific temperature ranges and require a particular climate to produce quality fruit. As you navigate the pages ahead, you'll discover the profound impact of climate on grape cultivation.

Microclimates, regional variations, and the dance between warmth and coolness all influence grape flavors and characteristics. Understanding the climate of your chosen grape-growing area is akin to knowing the secrets of the vineyard, and it's essential for success.

1.5 Soil Preparation

Now, let's dig into the earthy side of grapevine cultivation—soil preparation. Just as a chef selects the finest ingredients for a gourmet meal, a viticulturist carefully tends to the soil to create the perfect environment for grapevines.

Soil types vary widely, from sandy soils that drain quickly to clay soils that retain moisture. Each soil type has its own character, and understanding your soil's personality is crucial for the well-being of your grapevines.

Proper soil analysis and preparation ensure that your grapevines receive the essential nutrients they need to thrive. It's like laying the foundation for a sturdy house, and in this case, your house is a bountiful vineyard.

Chapter 2: Grapevine Planting and Training

2.1 Site Selection and Preparation

Welcome to Chapter 2, where we dive into the essential aspects of grapevine planting and training. As *a farmer, Sommelier, Gourmet, and Grapevine Breeder*, I understand the critical role that site selection and preparation play in crafting exceptional grapes and wines.

Site selection is like choosing the perfect canvas for a masterpiece. The location of your vineyard determines the quality and character of your grapes. Factors like sunlight exposure, soil composition, and drainage should be carefully considered when selecting a site. The right foundation sets the stage for success.

2.2 Planting Grapevines

Now, let's get our hands in the soil and talk about planting grapevines. It's the moment when potential transforms into reality. Planting grapevines requires precision and care, much like crafting a fine wine.

Spacing between vines, planting depth, and choosing the right grapevine varieties are all critical decisions. Your choice of trellis system should also be made before planting to ensure proper support for your vines. Each vine you plant is a step towards a fruitful future.

2.3 Training Systems

Training systems are the architectural framework that shapes your grapevines. As you embark on this section, think of yourself as both an artist and an engineer. Different training systems offer unique advantages, and your choice will impact vine health and grape quality.

Vertical shoot positioning (VSP), Scott Henry, or pergola systems—each has its strengths. They influence canopy management, sunlight exposure, and airflow around the vines. Mastering these systems is like conducting an orchestra; every element must harmonize for the best results.

2.4 Pruning Techniques

Pruning is the gentle art of shaping grapevines. It's a bit like sculpting a masterpiece. Pruning not only controls vine growth but also directs energy to where it's needed most—grape clusters. Different pruning techniques, such as spur pruning and cane pruning, offer varying levels of control and influence on the vine's growth.

Pruning may seem daunting at first, but with practice, it becomes an intuitive process. Your pruning decisions will affect grape yield, quality, and overall vine health. Think of it as a conversation with your vines, where you gently guide them towards greatness.

2.5 Trellising and Support Structures

Support structures, like trellises, are the unsung heroes of your vineyard. They provide stability, facilitate airflow, and make vineyard operations more manageable. Imagine them as the scaffolding that supports a grand building; they hold the key to a thriving vineyard.

Choosing the right trellis system—whether it's a Geneva Double Curtain or a High-Wire Cordon—depends on your training system and vineyard layout. Your trellising decisions will impact vine growth, fruit exposure, and ease of maintenance. They are the silent partners in your viticultural journey, ensuring your grapes reach their full potential.

Chapter 3: Grapevine Care and Maintenance

3.1 Watering and Irrigation

Welcome to Chapter 3, where we explore the crucial aspects of grapevine care and maintenance. As *a farmer, Sommelier, Gourmet, and Grapevine Breeder*, I understand that nurturing grapevines is a delicate balance of art and science. Let's begin with the life-giving element: water.

Watering and irrigation are fundamental to grapevine health. Grapes are sensitive to moisture levels, and inadequate or excessive watering can affect vine growth and grape quality. Understanding your vineyard's water needs, soil type, and climate is vital.

Modern irrigation systems offer precision and control, allowing you to tailor water delivery to your vines' specific requirements. Whether it's drip irrigation, soaker hoses, or traditional methods, a well-thought-out watering strategy ensures that your grapevines thrive.

3.2 Fertilization and Nutrient Management

Nutrition plays a crucial role in the well-being of grapevines. Just as a gourmet meal requires the finest ingredients, grapevines need essential nutrients to flourish. Fertilization and nutrient management are the keys to a healthy vineyard.

Soil analysis guides your fertilization strategy, helping you provide the right nutrients at the right time. Nitrogen, phosphorus, potassium, and micronutrients are essential for vine growth and grape development. Balanced nutrition leads to robust vines and flavorful grapes.

As a Grapevine Breeder, you'll appreciate that nutrient management is both an art and a science. It's about optimizing nutrient uptake while avoiding excesses that can harm your vines. A well-fed vineyard yields grapes that reflect the terroir and make exceptional wines.

3.3 Pest and Disease Control

Grapes, like fine wines, can be vulnerable to pests and diseases. Managing these challenges requires vigilance and expertise. Effective pest and disease control are essential for safeguarding your grapevines.

Common grape pests include aphids, grapevine moths, and leafhoppers. Diseases like powdery mildew and downy mildew can also threaten your crop. Integrated pest management (IPM) combines preventive measures, monitoring, and judicious use of pesticides to protect your vines.

As a farmer, you'll appreciate that a holistic approach is necessary. Promoting biodiversity in your vineyard, using natural predators, and monitoring pest populations are essential components of sustainable pest control. By carefully managing these challenges, you'll ensure your grapevines stay healthy and productive.

3.4 Weed Management

Weeds are like unwanted guests in your vineyard, competing for resources and space. Effective weed management is essential to maintain a thriving vineyard ecosystem.

Options for weed management include mechanical cultivation, mulching, and herbicides. Each method has its advantages and considerations. The choice depends on your vineyard's specific needs and your commitment to sustainable practices.

As a Grapevine Breeder, you'll recognize that weed management is more than just clearing the ground; it's about fostering a balanced vineyard environment. A weed-free vineyard not only looks tidy but also ensures that your grapevines receive the nutrients and attention they deserve.

3.5 Canopy Management

Canopy management is like grooming a prized vineyard, ensuring that your grapevines receive the right amount of sunlight and air circulation. It's an art that enhances grape quality and vine health.

Pruning, shoot thinning, and leaf removal are techniques that shape the vine canopy. These practices influence grape ripening, disease prevention, and overall vineyard aesthetics. The goal is to strike the perfect balance between shade and sunlight.

As a farmer, you'll recognize that canopy management is about orchestrating the symphony of your vineyard. It's a dynamic process that evolves throughout the growing season. By mastering this art, you'll craft grapes that reflect the true essence of your vineyard's terroir.

Chapter 4: Grape Harvesting and Post-Harvest Handling

4.1 Determining Ripeness

Welcome to Chapter 4, where we delve into the exciting world of grape harvesting and post-harvest handling. As *a farmer, Sommelier, Gourmet, and Grapevine Breeder*, I understand that this phase is where the magic happens. Let's begin by determining the moment of perfection: ripeness.

Ripeness is the heart and soul of grape harvesting. It's the stage when grapes reach their peak flavor, sugar content, and acidity. Determining ripeness is both a science and an art. Brix levels, pH, and taste tests all play a role in the decision-making process.

As a Grapevine Breeder, you'll appreciate that patience is key. Harvesting too early or too late can significantly impact wine quality. It's a delicate dance between timing and intuition, resulting in grapes that shine in the glass.

4.2 Harvesting Techniques

Harvesting is the moment of truth, where the fruits of your labor are gathered. The choice of harvesting technique depends on your goals and grape variety. Hand-picking offers precision and care, while mechanical harvesting is efficient for large vineyards.

As a farmer, you'll know that the right technique can make or break the harvest. Hand-harvesting allows for selective picking, ensuring that only the ripest grapes are collected. Mechanical harvesting, on the other hand, is suitable for grapes destined for certain wine styles.

Harvesting is a celebration of the vineyard's bounty, a culmination of months of hard work.

Whether by hand or machine, each grape is a testament to your dedication as a viticulturist.

4.3 Grape Sorting and Crushing

With the harvest complete, it's time to move to the next phase: grape sorting and crushing. This stage is a crucial step in ensuring the quality of your wine. Sorting separates the gems from the imperfections, while crushing releases the juice and skins.

Sorting can be done manually or mechanically, with each grape examined for ripeness and health. Crushing, whether by foot or machine, gently breaks the grapes to extract the juice. The choice of method depends on your winemaking style and equipment.

As a Sommelier, you'll appreciate the significance of this stage. The quality of grapes and the care taken in sorting and crushing directly impact the wine's flavor and aroma. It's a dance that sets the stage for winemaking excellence.

4.4 Fermentation and Winemaking

Fermentation is where grape juice transforms into wine, a magical alchemy that takes place in tanks or barrels. It's a process that combines science, tradition, and the winemaker's touch.

Yeast, whether wild or cultured, plays a pivotal role in fermentation, converting sugars into alcohol. Temperature control, punch-downs, and pump-overs are techniques used to manage the process. The length of fermentation varies, depending on the wine style.

As a Gourmet, you'll savor the intricate flavors and aromas that emerge during fermentation. Each decision made by the winemaker—from yeast selection to fermentation temperature—

shapes the wine's character. It's a journey of transformation and discovery.

4.5 Storage and Bottling

After fermentation, the wine enters a period of rest and maturation in barrels or tanks. This stage allows flavors to develop and textures to soften. The choice of oak, aging duration, and blending decisions are all part of the winemaker's craft.

As storage progresses, the winemaker monitors the wine's progress, occasionally tasting and testing. Once the wine has matured to perfection, it's time for bottling. This is where the finished product is sealed, ready to be enjoyed.

As a Grapevine Breeder, you'll appreciate that the journey doesn't end with harvest; it continues in the bottle. The art of winemaking involves patience and expertise, ensuring that each bottle tells a unique story of the vineyard's terroir and the winemaker's vision.

Chapter 5: Wine Production and Quality

5.1 The Art of Winemaking

Welcome to Chapter 5, where we explore the captivating world of wine production and quality. As *a farmer, Sommelier, Gourmet, and Grapevine Breeder*, I understand that winemaking is an exquisite blend of science and art. Let's begin with the heart of it all: the art of winemaking.

Winemaking is an age-old craft that has been refined and perfected over centuries. It involves a symphony of decisions, from grape selection to fermentation techniques. The winemaker's palate and intuition are as important as laboratory analysis.

As a Gourmet, you'll appreciate the craftsmanship that goes into every bottle. Winemakers create unique expressions of terroir, using their expertise to coax the best from each vintage. It's a pursuit of perfection that results in wines that delight the senses.

5.2 Factors Affecting Wine Quality

Wine quality is a complex interplay of factors, from the vineyard to the bottle. Understanding these factors is essential for producing exceptional wines. Grape variety, terroir, climate, and viticultural practices all leave their mark on the final product.

Winemaking decisions, such as fermentation temperature, aging vessel, and blending, also shape wine quality. Oxygen exposure, sulfur levels, and pH can significantly impact a wine's flavor and stability. Each choice contributes to the wine's unique personality.

As a Sommelier, you'll relish the diversity of wines produced worldwide, each a reflection of its origin and maker. Wine quality is a pursuit that never ends, as winemakers and enthusiasts alike seek to explore new dimensions of flavor and complexity.

5.3 Fermentation and Aging

Fermentation and aging are the transformative stages of winemaking, where grape juice becomes a living work of art. Fermentation, whether in stainless steel tanks or oak barrels, is where yeast performs its magic.

Aging in barrels or tanks allows wines to develop complexity and character. Oak aging imparts flavors of vanilla, spice, and toast, while time on lees can enhance texture and mouthfeel. The choice of vessel and duration of aging depend on the winemaker's vision.

As a Grapevine Breeder, you'll understand that patience is the key to excellence. The journey from grape to glass is marked by decisions that impact a wine's structure and aroma. The result is a testament to the winemaker's vision and the vineyard's terroir.

5.4 Blending and Flavor Profiles

Blending is where winemakers become artists, crafting wines with precise flavor profiles. Different grape varieties and vineyard blocks contribute unique elements to the blend. The goal is to create a harmonious wine that showcases the best of each component.

Blending allows winemakers to balance acidity, sweetness, tannins, and fruitiness. It's a delicate process of trial and error, guided by the winemaker's palate and experience. The result is a wine that tells a compelling story.

As a farmer, you'll appreciate that each vintage brings its challenges and opportunities.

Blending is a way to adapt to changing conditions and create consistent wines that capture the essence of the vineyard.

5.5 Wine Tasting and Evaluation

Finally, we arrive at the delightful stage of wine tasting and evaluation. It's where wine enthusiasts, professionals, and curious individuals come together to savor the fruits of labor. Tasting involves more than just sipping; it's an exploration of aroma, flavor, texture, and balance.

Wine evaluation includes assessing appearance, aroma, taste, and finish. Descriptors like fruity, floral, oaky, or spicy are used to capture the wine's essence. Each wine has its unique personality, and the art of tasting lies in appreciating its nuances.

As a Gourmet, you'll cherish the moments when wine opens up and reveals its secrets. Wine tasting is a lifelong journey, one that deepens your appreciation for the craftsmanship and diversity of wines. It's a journey worth savoring, one glass at a time.

Chapter 6: Sustainable Grape Farming Practices

6.1 Organic Viticulture

Welcome to Chapter 6, where we explore the world of sustainable grape farming practices. As *a farmer, Sommelier, Gourmet, and Grapevine Breeder*, I believe that sustainable practices are not just responsible but essential for the future of viticulture. Let's start with organic viticulture.

Organic viticulture is a holistic approach that prioritizes the health of the vineyard ecosystem. It eliminates synthetic pesticides and chemical fertilizers, relying instead on natural methods to maintain vine health. Organic practices promote biodiversity and soil fertility.

In my opinion, organic viticulture isn't just about what's left out; it's about what's embraced. It's a celebration of nature's wisdom and a commitment to producing grapes and wines that are in harmony with the environment. Choosing organic methods is a step towards a more sustainable and flavorful future.

6.2 Biodynamic Farming

Biodynamic farming takes sustainable viticulture a step further. It's a holistic and spiritual approach that considers the vineyard as a living entity. Biodynamic practices follow a lunar calendar and involve preparations made from natural materials.

As a Grapevine Breeder, you may appreciate the philosophy behind biodynamic farming. It goes beyond scientific methods, emphasizing the interconnectedness of all elements in the vineyard. Biodynamic practices aim to enhance the vineyard's vitality and produce grapes that express their terroir with unparalleled clarity.

Biodynamic farming might seem unconventional, but it's a testament to the diversity of approaches in viticulture. It invites us to explore a deeper connection with the land and the vines.

6.3 Integrated Pest Management

Integrated Pest Management (IPM) is a science-based approach to pest control that minimizes the impact on the environment. It involves monitoring pest populations, using natural predators, and employing targeted pesticide applications when necessary.

IPM is like a finely tuned orchestra, where pests are kept in check without harming beneficial organisms. It's a pragmatic approach that considers the complexities of the vineyard ecosystem.

As a farmer, you'll find IPM to be a practical and effective strategy for pest control. It allows you to protect your grapevines while minimizing the use of chemicals. It's a win-win for both the vineyard and the environment.

6.4 Soil Health and Biodiversity

Soil health is the foundation of sustainable viticulture. Healthy soil teems with life, supporting beneficial microorganisms and nutrient availability. Practices like cover cropping, composting, and minimal tillage are key to maintaining soil vitality.

Biodiversity in the vineyard is not just about grapevines; it's about creating a thriving ecosystem. Planting cover crops, preserving natural habitats, and encouraging beneficial insects all contribute to a biodiverse vineyard.

As a Sommelier, you may appreciate that healthy soils and biodiversity translate into wines that truly express their terroir. The flavors and nuances found in such wines are a testament to the richness of the vineyard's ecosystem.

6.5 Certification and Standards

Certification and standards help consumers identify and support sustainable vineyards and wineries. Organizations like organic and biodynamic certification bodies set guidelines and conduct audits to ensure compliance.

As a Gourmet, you can look for certification labels on wine bottles to make informed choices that align with your values. These labels provide assurance that the grapes were grown using sustainable practices, creating wines that are not only delicious but also responsible choices.

Sustainable grape farming practices, in my opinion, are a commitment to a future where vineyards flourish, wines delight, and the earth thrives. They are a testament to our responsibility as stewards of the land and our dedication to crafting wines that reflect the true beauty of nature.

Chapter 7: Challenges and Solutions in Grapevine Cultivation

7.1 Climate Change and Viticulture

Welcome to Chapter 7, where we confront the challenges and seek solutions in the world of grapevine cultivation. As *a farmer, Sommelier, Gourmet, and Grapevine Breeder*, it's vital to address the pressing issue of climate change and its impact on viticulture.

Climate change is altering the traditional grape-growing regions and introducing new challenges. Rising temperatures, altered rainfall patterns, and increased extreme weather events can disrupt grape production. Adaptation strategies like changing grape varieties and adjusting harvest times are crucial.

In my opinion, addressing climate change requires collective action. Farmers, winemakers, and consumers all play a role in reducing the carbon footprint of the wine industry. Sustainable practices, from vineyard to bottle, are vital in mitigating the effects of climate change and preserving the art of winemaking.

7.2 Disease Resistance and Genetic Research

Disease resistance is an ongoing challenge in grapevine cultivation. Fungal diseases like powdery mildew and downy mildew can devastate vineyards. Genetic research and breeding programs aim to develop disease-resistant grape varieties, reducing the need for chemical interventions.

As a Grapevine Breeder, you'll appreciate the potential of genetic research to create resilient grapevines. Disease-resistant varieties not only protect vineyards but also contribute to sustainable viticulture. It's a testament to the marriage of science and tradition in the world of grapes and wine.

Collaboration between researchers, farmers, and the wine industry is essential in advancing disease-resistant grape varieties. It's a shared commitment to preserving the future of grape cultivation.

7.3 Market Trends and Challenges

The wine market is dynamic, shaped by evolving consumer preferences and global trends. From natural wines to sustainability certifications, staying attuned to market demands is essential. Challenges may include navigating complex regulations, competition, and changing consumer expectations.

As a Gourmet, you'll recognize that market trends influence the availability and variety of wines. Supporting sustainable and ethical practices is a choice that resonates with many consumers today. It's a reflection of the changing landscape of wine appreciation.

Adapting to market trends while maintaining the integrity of your vineyard and wines requires creativity and flexibility. It's an opportunity to connect with consumers who appreciate the dedication and craftsmanship behind each bottle.

7.4 Labor and Machinery

Labor and machinery are pivotal in grapevine cultivation. Finding skilled labor and managing the costs associated with manual labor can be challenging. Machinery, on the other hand, can enhance efficiency but requires investment and expertise.

As a farmer, you'll understand the delicate balance between human expertise and mechanization. Modern technology, from pruning machines to harvesters, can streamline vineyard operations. Yet, the human touch remains indispensable in caring for grapevines.

Investing in training and machinery can optimize labor while maintaining the quality of grapes. It's a testament to the adaptability and innovation that have characterized the wine industry throughout history.

7.5 Economic Viability

Economic viability is at the core of grapevine cultivation. Sustainable practices, market trends, and labor costs all factor into the financial health of a vineyard. Ensuring economic sustainability while preserving the art of winemaking is a delicate balancing act.

In my opinion, economic viability is inseparable from sustainable practices. Efficient resource management and market responsiveness are key to a vineyard's success. A commitment to quality and environmental responsibility can also enhance a vineyard's brand and marketability.

Ultimately, economic viability is a reflection of the dedication and passion of those involved in grapevine cultivation. It's an enduring commitment to crafting wines that not only delight the senses but also ensure the longevity of this timeless tradition.

Chapter 8: Future of Grapevine Cultivation

8.1 Innovations in Grape Farming

Welcome to the final chapter, where we explore the exciting future of grapevine cultivation. As *a farmer, Sommelier, Gourmet, and Grapevine Breeder*, I'm eager to delve into the innovations that will shape the way we grow and enjoy grapes in the years to come.

Innovations in grape farming encompass a wide range of advancements. From precision viticulture using drones and sensors to data-driven decision-making, technology is revolutionizing the way we manage vineyards. These innovations improve efficiency, reduce environmental impact, and enhance grape quality.

In my opinion, embracing these innovations is not just about staying ahead in the industry; it's about responsible stewardship of the land. Sustainable farming practices and innovative technologies can go hand in hand, ensuring that future generations can enjoy the beauty of vineyards.

8.2 Emerging Grape Varieties

Emerging grape varieties are a testament to the dynamism of viticulture. As climate patterns shift, new grape varieties are gaining recognition for their adaptability and unique flavor profiles. These varieties offer exciting opportunities for experimentation and flavor discovery.

As a Gourmet, you'll relish the chance to explore wines crafted from these emerging varieties. They bring diversity to the wine world, showcasing the richness of different terroirs and the creativity of winemakers. It's an invitation to expand your palate and discover new favorites.

Embracing emerging grape varieties is a way to adapt to changing conditions and preserve the art of winemaking. It's a reminder that innovation is not limited to technology but extends to the very grapes that form the foundation of our beloved wines.

8.3 Sustainability and Market Demands

Sustainability is no longer a choice; it's a necessity in grapevine cultivation. Market demands for environmentally friendly and ethically produced wines are on the rise. Sustainable practices, from organic farming to carbon neutrality, are essential to meeting these demands.

As a Sommelier, you'll appreciate that sustainability is not just a buzzword; it's a commitment to quality and responsibility. Wineries that embrace sustainability are not only preserving the planet but also crafting wines that resonate with today's conscientious consumers.

Meeting market demands while maintaining sustainability is a win-win for both the wine industry and the environment. It's a testament to the industry's ability to adapt and evolve while upholding the values of craftsmanship and responsibility.

8.4 Global Wine Industry Trends

The global wine industry is ever-evolving. Trends like natural wines, wine tourism, and virtual tastings are shaping the way we experience wine. Understanding and adapting to these trends is essential for staying relevant and thriving in the wine world.

As a Grapevine Breeder, you'll recognize that the wine industry is a dynamic and interconnected ecosystem. Trends that emerge in one part of the world can influence practices globally. It's an exciting time to be a part of an industry that celebrates diversity and innovation.

Embracing global wine industry trends is a way to connect with wine enthusiasts worldwide. It's an opportunity to share experiences, knowledge, and the sheer joy of wine in all its forms.

8.5 Conclusion and Looking Ahead

As we conclude our journey through the world of grapevine cultivation, I want to express my gratitude for joining me on this exploration. The future of grapevine cultivation is bright and promising, filled with innovation, diversity, and sustainability.

As *a farmer, Sommelier, Gourmet, and Grapevine Breeder*, I am inspired by the resilience and passion of those who tend to the vineyards and craft the wines we cherish. The art of winemaking is an ever-evolving story, and each bottle is a chapter waiting to be savored.

As we look ahead, let us embrace the challenges and opportunities that come our way. Let us celebrate the beauty of vineyards, the diversity of grapes, and the joy of sharing a glass of wine with friends and loved ones. The future of grapevine cultivation is in our hands, and together, we can raise our glasses to a world of possibilities.